T0011567

THE LITTLE BOOK OF
SCOTLAND

This edition published in 2023 by OH!
An Imprint of Welbeck Non-Fiction Limited,
part of Welbeck Publishing Group.
Offices in: London – 20 Mortimer Street, London W1T 3JW
and Sydney – Level 17, 207 Kent St, Sydney NSW 2000 Australia
www.welbeckpublishing.com

ISBN 978-1-80069-401-9

Compiled and written by: Isobel Reid
Editorial: Catriona Smith
Project manager: Russell Porter
Design: Tony Seddon
Production: Jess Brisley

A CIP catalogue record for this book is available from the British Library

Printed in China

10 9 8 7 6 5 4 3 2 1

THE LITTLE BOOK OF
SCOTLAND

LAND OF LOCHS AND LEGENDS

CONTENTS

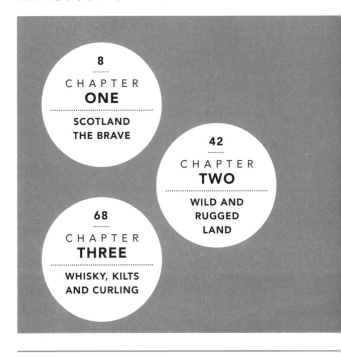

INTRODUCTION

With its soaring peaks, breathtaking lochs and glens, rich lore and traditions, and warm and welcoming people, Scotland – the most northerly of the four countries that make up the United Kingdom – is consistently ranked as one of the world's most beautiful and best-loved travel destinations.

A rich and complex history has shaped Scotland into the nation it is today. From ancient tombs and monuments to brooding medieval castles and the very modern Scottish Parliament building that stands proudly at the foot of Edinburgh's Royal Mile, the country's diverse landmarks reveal its fascinating and often turbulent history. It's a story of invading Romans and Vikings, of powerful clansmen and kings, of fierce battles for independence, and of the "Scottish Enlightenment" – an extraordinary period in the 18th and 19th centuries when the country's scientists, philosophers, writers and artists made incredible advances that shaped the modern world.

Scotland may be part of the United Kingdom, but a proud and distinct identity unites the country. For more than a thousand years, each generation has added its own unique thumbprint to create the country's rich cultural landscape. From whisky distilleries and legendary golf courses to kilts, ceildihs and "tossing the caber", Scotland's "brand" is famous the world over. And then there's the landscape. From the rolling hills and fertile farmland of the Lowlands to the raw, magnificent scenery of the Highlands and the remote Islands, Scotland is a land of staggering natural beauty.

Packed full of historical facts, quirky asides, and wise and witty quotes, *The Little Book of Scotland* captures the nation at its glorious best. Covering everything from majestic munros, crumbling castles and mysterious legends to culture-rich cities, architectural wonders and great Scots – not to mention haggis, whisky and wild weather – it's a wonderful celebration of this vibrant and extraordinary land.

CHAPTER
ONE

SCOTLAND THE BRAVE

Scotland's rich and fascinating history is peppered with conquests, battles, drama and intrigue.

From the fierce Picts who defied the Romans to proud clansmen, powerful rulers and the extraordinary scientists and thinkers of the Age of Enlightenment, the country's turbulent past has shaped the nation it is today.

Hundreds of millions of years ago, Scotland's landmass was separated from England and Wales by the ancient Iapetus Ocean – in fact, it was joined to America and Greenland.

When the first
modern humans
ventured from Africa,
more than 50,000 years
ago, Scotland was still
covered with a thick
layer of ice. The first
hunter gatherers did
not arrive there until
12,000 BCE.

Around 6,100 BCE
a giant, 21-metre
(70-foot) tsunami
devastated coastal
communities in the
Shetland Islands and
eastern Scotland.

Between 4,000 BCE and 2,000 BCE, Scotland's inhabitants built chambered tombs to honour their dead, and spectacular monuments, such as circles of standing stones.

Three Ancient Monuments

Maeshowe is a stone-built, chambered tomb near Stromness in the Orkney islands. On the winter solstice, the sun shines directly down the entrance passageway, flooding the main chamber with light.

On the Isle of Lewis, overlooking the waters of Loch Roag, are the mysterious **Calanais Standing Stones**. No one is sure what stone circles were used for, but they may have been used for astronomical observations and religious rituals.

Orkney's remarkable settlement of **Skara Brae** dates back to 3,200 BCE. The houses, connected by covered passageways, have stone beds and seats.

The site was discovered in the winter of 1850, when a great storm ripped the earth and grass from a large mound known as Skerrabra.

In the first century CE, Britain was invaded by the Romans. The southern part became the Roman province of Britannia, but Britain's northern tribes could not be subdued.

To stop these tribes from invading Britannia, Emperor Hadrian built a massive wall across the island, from east to west. Part of Hadrian's Wall still stands on the Scottish border today.

❝

[The Romans]
make a desert and
call it 'peace'.

❞

The Celtic chieftain Calgacus, who fought the Romans
at the Battle of Mons Graupius in 83 or 84 CE. This is
the first recorded statement by a "Scot".

The Romans called
the land north of
Hadrian's Wall
Caledonia. Its people
were called Picts,
from the Latin *pictus* –
meaning "painted".

Hadrian's death in 138 CE brought a new Roman emperor, Antoninus Pius, to power. He abandoned Hadrian's Wall and moved the frontier up to the Forth–Clyde isthmus, where he built a new turf wall – the Antonine Wall.

From Old Kilpatrick on the west coast to near Bo'ness in the east, it was around 37 miles (60 km) long.

According to tradition, Christianity reached Scotland in 400 CE when Saint Ninian led a mission to convert the Picts.

In the sixth century, the Irish abbot Saint Columba established a monastic community on the tiny island of Iona.

Located in the Inner
Hebrides, Iona is just
3 miles (5 km) long.
Known as the "Cradle of
Christianity" in Scotland,
the beautiful island
draws more than 130,000
visitors each year.

The Vikings first arrived in Scotland in the early ninth century. Initially, they were raiders, looting and stealing precious objects.

Later, they came as traders and settlers, colonizing areas such as the northern islands of Orkney and Shetland, the Hebrides, and mainland areas such as Sutherland and Caithness.

Three Viking Sites

Jarlshof, Shetland – The Norse settlement at Jarlshof originated in the 9th century, with the earliest longhouse used over successive generations.

Scar boat burial, Orkney – The remains of a man, woman and 10-year-old child were discovered near the village of Scar. They were buried with a sword, arrows, a whalebone plaque and other items.

The Isle of Lewis – In 1831, 93 chessmen, carved out of walrus and whales' teeth, were found on the beach at Uig. They were likely made in Norway, between 1150 and 1200.

In 900 CE, the Kingdom of Alba was founded by the Picts and the Celts.

Its first king was Kenneth MacAlpin – though much of the story of his life and reign is shrouded in legend.

Alba's most famous king, Macbeth – forever immortalized by Shakespeare – ruled Alba from 1040 to 1057. He was credited with expanding the kingdom's borders, but his reign was also marked by violence and civil unrest.

He was eventually overthrown and killed by Malcolm III, the son of Duncan I – the king he had murdered in order to gain the throne.

In 1296, England's Edward I sacked the Scottish trading port of Berwick-Upon-Tweed and stripped the king, John Balliol, of his royal vestments.

In response, the Scottish knight William Wallace and esquire Andrew Moray raised an army of Scots and inflicted a decisive defeat over a strong English army at the Battle of Stirling Bridge.

66

I am William Wallace, and the rest of you will be spared. Go back to England and tell them there that Scotland's daughters and her sons are yours no more. Tell them Scotland is free!

99

From the film *Braveheart*, 1995

Scotland's fight for independence continued into the 14th century. At the Battle of Bannockburn in 1314, Robert the Bruce and his army defeated England's Edward II.

In 1320, the Declaration of Arbroath, a letter in Latin signed by Scottish barons and nobles, was sent to Pope John XXII proclaiming Scotland's status as an independent sovereign state.

66

We fight not for glory
nor for wealth nor
honours; but only
and alone we fight for
freedom, which no
good man surrenders
but with his life.

99

**Bernard de Linton, from The Declaration
of Arbroath, 1320**

Perhaps Scotland's most famous figure, Mary Stuart was just six days old when she became Queen of Scots in 1542. Her reign was marked by Catholic-Protestant conflict and civil unrest.

Worried about a Catholic plot against her, Elizabeth I , Queen of England and Ireland, imprisoned her cousin Mary and had her beheaded 19 years later, at the age of 44.

"

En ma Fin gît mon
Commencement.
('In my End is my
Beginning'.)

"

**The words that Mary Queen of Scots embroidered
on her cloth of estate whilst imprisoned in England
by Elizabeth I.**

James VI, the son of Mary, Queen of Scots, succeeded the throne at just 13 months old after his mother was forced to abdicate. When Elizabeth I died with no children, James VI succeeded to the English throne and became James VI & I.

This historic event, in 1603, is known as the **Union of the Crowns**.

In 1688, William of Orange
invaded England to overthrow
King James VII – an event
that would lead to decades of
bloodshed.

James VII fled to France,
and his supporters – the
Jacobites – battled to restore
him to the throne.

In 1745, James VII's grandson Prince Charles Edward Stuart – better known as Bonnie Prince Charlie – arrived in Scotland to regain the British throne on behalf of his father, James Stuart.

However, the Jacobite cause came to a tragic end at the Battle of Culloden – the last battle fought on British soil – when around 1,300 Highlanders were slain in a single hour.

66

Their winding-sheet the
bluidy clay,
Their graves are growin'
green to see;
And by them lies the dearest lad
That ever blest a woman's e'e!

99

**From "The Lovely Lass O' Inverness" by Robert Burns,
which alludes to the bloodshed that unfolded at the
Battle of Culloden.**

Following the Battle of Culloden, a series of laws were introduced to prevent another Jacobite uprising. Clans such as Mackintosh and Campbell had ruled their lands for hundreds of years, but the Highland Clearances changed all that.

Thousands of highlanders were evicted from their land and forced to emigrate, many of them to Britain's new colonies in Canada, Australia, and New Zealand.

In the 18th and 19th centuries,
The Age of Enlightenment
saw Scottish thinkers and
scientists – such as Robert
Burns, David Hume, William
Cullen, Sir Walter Scott and
Adam Smith – develop ideas
that would change the way we
relate to the modern world.

The movement ranged across
geology, engineering, chemistry,
poetry, medicine and history,
but at its heart was philosophy.

"

Edinburgh is a hotbed of genius.

"

Tobias Smollett, 18th-century Scottish poet

66

Of all the small
nations of this
earth, perhaps only
the ancient Greeks
surpass the Scots in
their contribution
to mankind.

99

Winston Churchill

In 1999, a new era for the Scottish people was ushered in as the Scottish Parliament reconvened for the first time in almost 300 years. This saw the granting of certain powers and increased self-governance for Scotland.

In 2004, the Scottish Parliament building opened at Holyrood in Edinburgh.

In September 2014, a referendum was held on Scottish independence.

In response to the question, "Should Scotland be an independent country", **1,617,989 (45%)** voted Yes and **2,001,926 (55%)** voted No.

CHAPTER
TWO

WILD AND RUGGED LAND

From the gentle, rolling countryside of the Lowlands to the wild and rugged terrain of the Highlands, Scotland's landscape is a stunning tapestry of soaring peaks, forests and moorlands, tranquil lochs and dramatic coastlines.

A haven for wildlife, the country's unrivalled landscapes attract visitors from around the globe, and have long been celebrated in art, literature and music.

66

O Caledonia! stern and wild,
Meet nurse for a poetic child!
Land of brown heath and shaggy wood,
Land of the mountain and the flood,
Land of my sires! what mortal hand
Can e'er untie the filial band
That knits me to thy rugged strand!

99

Sir Walter Scott, from
"The Lay of the Last Minstrel", 1805

"

Give me but one
hour of Scotland,
let me see it ere
I die.

"

William Edmondstoune Aytoun

Scotland in Numbers

Scotland makes up a large part of
the British Isles and its size is roughly
equivalent to one-third of
the mainland.

Total area: 30,420 square miles
(78,789 sq km)

Coastline: 11,602 miles (18,672 km)

Population: Around 5.2 million

Density: 166 people per square mile
(64 per sq km)

(Figures include Scotland's islands)

66

Staring into a
Scottish landscape, I
have often asked myself
why – in spite of all
appearances – bracken,
rocks, man and sea are
at some level one.

99

Neal Ascherson, Scottish journalist and writer

Scotland has three
main parts: the **Lowlands**,
Highlands and **Islands**.

The Lowlands are known for
their farmland and dense
forests, the Highlands for their
spectacular mountains and
deep lochs, and the Islands for
their sweeping beaches and
magnificent sea views.

"

There are two
seasons in
Scotland: June
and winter.

"

Billy Connolly

There are two national parks in Scotland: **The Cairngorms National Park** and **Loch Lomond and the Trossachs National Park**.

In addition, numerous nature reserves have been set up to protect the country's land and wildlife.

66

Farewell to the Highlands,
farewell to the North,

The birth-place of Valour,
the country of Worth;

Wherever I wander,
wherever I rove,

The hills of the Highlands
for ever I love.

99

Robert Burns

Five Wild Places

1. Rannoch Moor

– With a relatively central location, this vast wilderness has an abundance of flora and fauna – and plenty of wild weather. Surrounded by brooding mountains, the challenging terrain is covered with lochs, lochans, peat bogs and streams.

2. St Kilda – This far-flung cluster of islands in the middle of the Atlantic was once populated but has been abandoned since the 1930s. It boasts some of the highest sea cliffs in Britain and is home to globally important colonies of gannets, fulmars and puffins.

3. The Isle of Rum – The island is an ancient extinct volcano with impressive mountains and beaches. It has one of the largest Manx shearwater colonies in the world, as well as nearly 1,000 deer and golden and white-tailed eagles.

4. Ardnamurchan – This stunning, unspoilt peninsula is known primarily for Sanna Bay and Ardtoe with their pristine white-sand beaches. Wild and remote, its Gaelic name means "headland of the great seas".

5. Cape Wrath – Few tourists reach this beguiling corner of Scotland – the country's most north-westerly point. It is a captivating wilderness with sea cliffs, glorious beaches and an array of wildlife.

"

My favourite climb
is St Kilda, west of
Benbecula in Scotland's
Outer Hebrides. It's
incredibly remote, with
the highest sea cliffs
in Britain.

"

Steve Backshall

66

let the sun beat
on our forgetfulness
one hour of all
the heat intense
and summer lightning
on the Kilpatrick hills

99

From "Strawberries", Edwin Morgan

John o' Groats is one of Scotland's most popular tourist destinations – a famous signpost marks it as the most northerly point on mainland Britain.

In truth, though, the most northerly point on Britain's mainland is Dunnet Head – 14 miles (23 km) west of John o' Groats.

The most northeasterly point on mainland Britain is Duncansby Head, a 30-minute walk along the coast from John o' Groats.

66

There is no sunlight in the poetry
of exile. There is only mist,
wind, rain, the cry of the curlew, and
the slow clouds above damp moorland.
That is the real Scotland; that is
the Scotland whose memory rings the
withers of the far-from-home;
and, in some way that is mysterious,
that is the Scotland that even a
stranger learns to love.

99

H. V. Morton

The UK's most remote pub is The Old Forge, situated in the small village of Inverie, on the south shore of the Knoydart Peninsula.

With no roads in or out, you'll need to take a boat from Mallaig (a 7-mile / 11-km journey), or hike for 18 miles (30 km) over munros.

> **"**
> There are few places in my life
> that I've found more ruggedly
> beautiful than the Highlands of
> Scotland. The place is magical —
> it's so far north, so remote, that
> sometimes it feels like you've left
> this world and gone to another.
> **"**

Julia London

Munro Bagging is the pursuit of climbing Scotland's munros.

Around 7,000 people, called "compleatists" (or Munroists) have climbed all 282.

Marilyn or Munro?

Name/Height	Number in Scotland
Marilyn Under 610 m (2,000 ft)	1,216
Donald Above 610 m (2,000 ft)	140
Graham 610-762 m (2,000-2,500 ft)	221
Corbett 762-914 m (2,500-3,000 ft)	221
Munro Over 914 m (3,000 ft)	282

Note: Donalds are situated in the Scottish Lowlands.

The highest peak in Scotland – and across the British Isles – is Ben Nevis.

Standing at 4,413 metres (1,345 feet) above sea level, snow may be seen on its summit all year round.

The peak is the collapsed dome of a volcano that imploded millions of years ago.

Walkers tackling the Ben
take an average of seven
or eight hours to the summit
and back.

Each September, the winner
of The Ben Race takes around
90 minutes to complete the
same route.

Loch is the Scottish Gaelic word for a body of water, either completely or almost completely surrounded by land. Scotland has more than 31,000 lochs – including smaller lochs, called lochans.

Scotland's watery landscapes were formed during the last ice age. Colossal sheets of ice spawned massive glaciers that rolled across the land and gouged out spectacular valleys.

Record-breaking Lochs

Loch Ness – the largest loch by volume
(7.4 km³ / 1.8 cubic miles)

Loch Morar – the deepest loch
(310 metres / 1,017 feet)

Loch Awe – the longest inland loch
(25 miles / 41 km)

Loch Lomond – the largest loch by
surface area (27.5 sq miles / 71 km²)

Loch Fyne – the longest sea loch
(43 miles / 70 km)

Northern Scotland is on the same latitude as parts of Norway and Alaska, and the Northern Lights can be seen on cold nights when the sky is free of clouds.

Five of the best places to spot these spectacular displays are:

Shetland
The Outer Hebrides
Orkney
Caithness
Skye

In Scottish Gaelic folklore, the Northern Lights are known as the *Na Fir Chlis* – "the Nimble Men" – as well as the "Mirrie Dancers" in Orkney and Shetland.

CHAPTER
THREE

WHISKY, KILTS AND CURLING

Scotland's tumultuous past is at the root of its art, literature, celebrations and national pride.

From the stirring sounds of the bagpipes or the mesmerizing rhythm of traditional ceilidh dancing to haggis, Hogmanay and the Highland Games, the country's rich and diverse culture is a treasure trove of history, legend and folklore.

66

We look to Scotland for all our ideas of civilization.

99

Voltaire

"

Did not strong connections draw me elsewhere, I believe Scotland would be the country I would choose to end my days in.

"

Benjamin Franklin

Scotland's (unofficial) national anthem, "Flower of Scotland", can't be properly played on the bagpipes because it contains a note – a flattened seventh – that the pipes cannot produce.

66

O Flower of Scotland,
When will we see
Your likes again,
That fought and died for,
Your wee bit Hill and Glen,
And stood against them,
Proud Edward's Army,
And sent them homeward,
Tae think again.

99

**The first verse from Scotland's "unofficial"
national anthem, "Flower of Scotland"**

10 Scottish Symbols

National symbol
The Scottish thistle

National flag
The Saltire (diagonal white cross on a blue background)

Unofficial flag
The Lion Rampant (red "rampant lion" on a gold background)

National Instrument
Bagpipes

National anthem
Scotland doesn't have
an official anthem, but
"Flower of Scotland" is the
most popular choice.

Patron Saint
St Andrew, said to be
one of Jesus' original apostles

National poet
Robert ("Rabbie")
Burns, 1759–96

National tree
Scots Pine (designated 2014)

National dress
Traditional Scottish kilt

Scottish Sayings

What's fur ye'll no go by ye.
"What's for you will not go past you"
– or "Hold onto your dreams".

Lang may yer lum reek!
"Long may your chimney smoke"
– a greeting to wish someone good
fortune and a long life.

Yer lookin' peely wally.
"You look a little unwell".

Mony a mickle maks a muckle!
"Little savings can make big amounts".

It's a dreich day!
"It's a miserable, wet day".

Haud yer wheesht!
"Be quiet!"

Keep the heid!
"Keep your head" or "Keep your cool".

Awa' an bile yer heid!
"Go and boil your head" – or "Get lost".

Whisky, the "water of life" (or "*uisge beatha*" in Gaelic) is one of Scotland's best-loved products.

Home to 130 whisky distilleries, Scotland has the highest concentration of whisky production in the world.

"

Being moderately taken, it cutteth fleume,
it lighteneth the mynd, it quickeneth
the spirits, it cureth the hydropsie, it
pounceth the stone, it repelleth gravel…
the teeth from chatterying, the throte
from rattlying, the weasan from stieflying,
the stomach from womblying, the harte
from swellying, the bellie from wirtching,
the guts from rumblying, the hands from
shivering… and truly it is a sovereign
liquor if it be orderlie taken.

"

**Raphael Holinshed on whisky in his *Chronicles of England,
Scotland and Ireland*, 1577**

66

I should never have switched from Scotch to Martinis.

99

Humphrey Bogart's reputed last words

66

A good gulp of hot
whisky at bedtime – it's
not very scientific,
but it helps.

99

**Alexander Fleming, the Scottish inventor of penicillin,
offers advice for treating a cold**

There are more than 20 million casks of maturing whisky in Scotland – almost four casks for every person in the country!

Scotland may be the world's biggest whisky producer – but the Scots don't drink the most Scotch whisky.

The three biggest importers (in bottles per year) are:

France – 176 million

India – 136 million

USA – 126 million

The world's oldest whisky – in terms of time spent aging in the cask – is a Macallan that's been maturing since 1940.

Distilled in 1940, "the Reach" was aged for 81 years before being bottled in 2021.

Each of the 288 bottles costs **$125,000**.

"

Astonishing depth [with]
notes of dark chocolate, sweet
cinnamon and aromatic peat,
leading on to treacle toffee,
crystalised ginger and charred
pineapple, before giving way to
an intensely rich, sweet
and smoky finish.

"

**Description of The Macallan the Reach whisky,
the oldest whisky in the world**

Scotland may be famous for its whisky – but did you know between 70 and 80 per cent of the UK's gin is produced in Scotland?

There are over 100 varieties to choose from, including the world-famous Hendrick's, and Islay's dry gin, made with 22 wild botanicals and 9 classic gin spices, The Botanist.

66

Be happy while
you're living, for
you're a long
time dead.

99

Scottish proverb

The word **kilt** comes from the ancient Norse word kjilt, meaning "pleated".

There is evidence that Scottish Highlanders wore tartan as early as the 16th century. The first kilts were white, brown, green or black – the wool was dyed with the help of plants, mosses and berries.

Tartans for specific clans were later developed with the colours based on nearby natural dyes. Today, Scotland has more than 7,000 different registered tartans.

Celebrated Clans

Scotland's clans (from the Gaelic *clann*, "children") date back to the 12th century.

Here are ten of the best known, along with their castle strongholds and mottos.

Clan Campbell – Inveraray Castle
Motto: "Forget Not"

Clan Macdonald – Castle Tioram
Motto: "By Sea and By Land"

Clan Macleod – Dunvegan Castle
Motto: "Hold Fast"

Clan Sinclair – Castle of Mey
Motto: "Commit Thy Work to God"

Clan Mackintosh – Rait Castle
Motto: "Touch Not the Cat
Without a Glove"

Clan Mackenzie – Eilean Donan
Motto: "I Shine, Not Burn"

Clan Douglas – Douglas Castle
Motto: "Never Behind"

Clan Maclean – Duart Castle
Motto: "Virtue Mine Honour"

Clan Macnab – Doune Castle
Motto: "Let Fear Be Far From All"

Clan Stewart – Edinburgh Castle
Motto: "Courage grows strong
at a wound"

Fast-paced and physically demanding, the sport of **shinty** – played with sticks and a ball – has been enjoyed in Scotland for hundreds of years.

It is most commonly played in the Scottish Highlands, but it also has a dedicated following in other parts of Scotland and around the world.

The traditional game of **curling** can be traced back to medieval times, with the world's oldest curling stone dating from 1511.

Henry Adamson, a Scottish historian and poet, is credited with coining the word "curling" in 1620.

The origin of the word **haggis** isn't known for sure, but it is thought to come from the Old Norse word *höggva*, meaning to cut or hit.

Haggis is made of sheep's heart, liver and lungs. The meat is minced and mixed with onion, oatmeal, suet, spices and salt. Then it is traditionally packed into a sheep's stomach and boiled.

For those who aren't fans of eating haggis, there's always haggis hurling – the sport of throwing haggis as far and as fast as you can.

Burns Night, celebrated annually on 25 January, marks the birth of Scotland's national poet, Robert ("Rabbie") Burns.

The first Burns supper was held in July 1801, when several of Burns' close friends got together to mark the anniversary of their friend's death.

A traditional Burns Supper includes haggis, "neeps" (turnips) and "tatties" (potatoes) – and, of course, several drams of good Scots whisky.

After the haggis is ceremoniously "piped in", the haggis is addressed with Burns' famous poem, "Address to a Haggis".

66

Fair fa' your honest, sonsie face,
Great Chieftain o' the Puddin-race!
Aboon them a' ye tak your place,
Painch, tripe, or thairm:
Weel are ye wordy of a grace
As lang's my arm.

99

*Translation: "Good luck to you and your honest, plump face /
Great chieftain of the sausage race! / Above them all you take
your place / Stomach, tripe or intestines / Well are you worthy
of a grace / As long as my arm."*

From "Address to a Haggis" by Robert Burns

Although the bagpipes are widely assumed to be a Scottish invention, their use dates back centuries, with references to them in Rome and Egypt.

Some historians believe the bagpipes were brought to Scotland by invading Roman legions, more than 2,000 years ago.

One of the first mentions of the bagpipes appears in 1549, at the **Battle of Pinkie**, when the pipes helped inspire the Highlanders into battle.

More than 350 years later, at the Battle of the Somme in 1916, a war correspondent described the powerful impact of the pipes as Highland regimental pipers went into battle. Afterwards, the pipers played a Scottish "love song" as a lament to fallen comrades.

"

Scotland has an in-built sound system that never stops thumping. Music runs deep and I like to think of all the great songs and voices that have come out of the country, and all the music that is yet to come.

"

KT Tunstall

Ceilidh is a Gaelic word meaning "gathering" or "party". Nowadays, ceilidhs – featuring Scottish folk music and dancing with jigs and reels – are often held on special occasions such as weddings.

In 2000, Edinburgh's Hogmanay celebrations were the site of the world record for the largest ceilidh dance when 1,914 people danced Strip the Willow.

Scotland is known around the world as the "home of golf" – and today, the country has the highest proportion of golf holes per capita in the world.

The town of St Andrews – with a population of just 18,000 – has 12 golf courses, while Aberdeen is home to more than 70 courses.

The word "golf" first appeared in an act of the Scots Parliament on 6 March 1457, during the reign of James II. The pastime was banned — along with football — with those partaking liable to be arrested by the king's officers.

The Old Links at Musselburgh Racecourse is generally considered to be the oldest golf course in the world.

Mary, Queen of Scots, reputedly played there in 1567.

An absolute must for any golf fan, the **Old Course at St Andrews** – also known as the "Old Lady" – is widely regarded as the spiritual home of golf. The first documented rounds of golf here date back to 1552.

The Open Championship, the oldest of golf's major championships, has been hosted here 30 times since 1873, most recently in 2022.

Great Scots!

Scotland has produced many movers and shakers over the course of its history.

The list is long – here are just eight:

Mary Somerville – A scientist, writer and polymath, she was the first person to be described in print as a "scientist".

Alexander Graham Bell – Credited with inventing the first telephone, he also made important contributions to the fields of speech therapy and aeronautics.

Adam Smith – Best known for his book *The Wealth of Nations*, Smith is considered one of the founding fathers of modern economics.

Sir Walter Scott – A pioneer in the historical novel genre, his works include *Ivanhoe* and *Waverley*.

Bessie Wallace – This 19th-century suffragette and social reformer fought for women's and workers' rights.

Robert Louis Stevenson – The novelist, poet, and travel writer is celebrated for works such as *Treasure Island* and *The Strange Case of Dr Jekyll and Mr Hyde*.

Alexander Fleming – His discovery of penicillin in 1928 revolutionized the treatment of bacterial infections.

J.M. Barrie – The playwright's *Peter Pan*, or "The Boy Who Wouldn't Grow Up" was first performed in 1904 and remains a beloved classic of children's literature.

Scotland's new year celebrations are called **Hogmanay**. Fireworks and street parties across the country last for three days – beginning at the end of December and ending on 2 January.

The word Hogmanay is thought to come from the French word *hoginane*, meaning "gala day".

First footing is the visiting of friends or family immediately after midnight on New Year's Eve.

Traditionally, your first footer should be a tall, dark-haired man. This is said to date back to the time of the Viking invasions, when blond, Scandinavian-looking men spelt danger!

First footers also traditionally bring a lump of coal to ensure your house remains warm in the coming months.

The **Highland Games** have been held in Scotland for more than 1,000 years.

Showcasing strongman competitions such as caber tossing, stone put and weight throwing, they also feature bagpipe playing and Scottish country dancing.

Tossing the caber is one of the Highland Games' most iconic events, where competitors toss a full-length log, or caber, into the air. But the toss is not about distance – the aim is for the caber to land in line with the original run.

If it is straight, the toss is said to be in the 12 o'clock position. Competitors are judged on how closely their toss lands to 12 o'clock.

CHAPTER
FOUR

CITIES AND SIGHTS

From beautiful Edinburgh, with its breathtaking views, and the vibrant city of Glasgow, with its dynamic arts scene, to the charming city of Inverness and the imposing "Granite City" of Aberdeen, Scotland's cities and towns are packed full of art, culture and history galore.

From captivating castles to iconic battlefields, this chapter brings you a taste of Scotland's most stirring sights.

Scotland is home to seven vibrant cities, each of which boasts its own unique character.

Aberdeen – "The Granite City"

Dundee – "City of the Three Js" (jute, jam and journalism)

Edinburgh – "Auld Reekie" (Old Smoky)

Glasgow – "Dear Green Place"

Inverness – "Capital of the Highlands"

Perth – "The Fair City"

Stirling – "Gateway to the Highlands"

Three Scottish cities are
UNESCO-recognized.

The capital, Edinburgh,
is a City of Literature;
Glasgow is a City of
Music; and Dundee is
a City of Design.

From the ninth century up until 1437, Perth was Scotland's capital city, and nearby Scone Palace was the crowning place for many Scottish kings and queens.

Perth is known as the "Fair City" because of Sir Walter Scott's 1828 novel, *The Fair Maid of Perth*.

The River Tay,
which flows through
Perth, is the longest
river in Scotland,
measuring
120 miles (193 km)
in length.

Scotland's ancient yet dynamic capital, Edinburgh, is famed for its striking architecture and dramatic cityscape.

A centre of culture and the arts, it is especially known for its festivals. These include the Edinburgh International Book Festival and the Edinburgh Fringe – the world's largest festival of the arts.

66

This is a city of shifting light, of changing skies, of sudden vistas. A city so beautiful it breaks the heart again and again.

99

Alexander McCall Smith on Edinburgh

Home to kings and queens for many centuries, Edinburgh Castle rises majestically above the city.

The rock on which the castle is built is the plug of a volcano, thought to be around 350 million years old.

One of the most embattled fortresses in Europe – and the most besieged place in the UK – Edinburgh Castle has seen off hostile forces no less than 23 times.

The annual Military Tattoo held at Edinburgh Castle features a spectacular display of music, dance and pageantry.

It is one of the largest and most famous military tattoos in the world, attracting thousands of visitors from all over the globe each year.

The celebrated Forth Bridge, which links Edinburgh to Fife by railway, was a milestone in civil engineering and was the first major structure in Britain to be made of steel. It still holds the record as the world's longest cantilever bridge.

Work on the foundations started in 1882 and the bridge was completed in 1889. At the peak of activity, about 4,600 men – known as "briggers" – were employed in building the structure.

66

Half a capital and half a country town, the whole city leads a double existence; it has long trances of the one and flashes of the other; like the king of the Black Isles, it is half alive and half a monumental marble.

99

Robert Louis Stevenson,
Edinburgh: Picturesque Notes, 1878

Top 10 Attractions in Edinburgh

Edinburgh Castle

Arthur's Seat

The Royal Mile

Royal Yacht Britannia

Royal Botanic Garden

Palace of Holyroodhouse

St Giles Cathedral

Scottish National Gallery and Portrait Gallery

The Real Mary King's Close

Calton Hill

Connecting Edinburgh
Castle with the Palace
of Holyrood, the
Royal Mile is Edinburgh's
most famous street.

But it isn't actually
a mile – it's 1.1 miles,
or a "Scots Mile".

St Andrews is home to the University of St Andrews, founded between 1410 and 1413.

It is the third oldest university in the English-speaking world and the oldest in Scotland.

The ruined medieval cathedral in St Andrews was once the largest church in Scotland and a major centre of pilgrimage and religious power.

Destroyed during the Scottish Reformation in the 16th century, its ruins now stand as a testament to Scotland's rich heritage.

Dominating a vast volcanic rock above the river Forth, **Stirling Castle** stands at the meeting point between the Lowlands and the Highlands.

During the Wars of Independence (1296–1357), the castle changed hands eight times between Scottish and English control.

Mary, Queen of Scots was crowned at Stirling Castle's royal chapel, and returned in her later years, when her son, James VI, took residence at the palace.

In 1981, a strange discovery was made during renovations at the castle. Behind the panelling of the queen's chamber, workers came across the oldest football ever discovered.

Made from a pig's bladder, it was wrapped in cow hide – and is about half the size of a modern football.

Scotland's biggest city, Glasgow, is Scotland's beating heart.

It was once one of the world's largest shipbuilding cities and referred to as the "Second City of the British Empire".

Glasgow has a rich cultural heritage, including its famous school of architecture, The Glasgow School, which produced prominent architects such as **Charles Rennie Mackintosh**. You can see many of his designs in attractions such as the Mackintosh at the Willow, The Lighthouse and House for an Art Lover.

Ten Things to See in Glasgow

1. George Square
The heart of Glasgow and the city's main square.

2. Glasgow Cathedral
This beautiful gothic cathedral is Glasgow's oldest building.

3. The Necropolis
A Victorian cemetery modelled on Père-Lachaise in Paris.

4. Buchanan Street
A bustling boulevard lined with an incredible number of shops.

5. The GoMA
A world-class museum of modern art.

6. The Riverside Museum
A fabulous transport museum built on a
former shipyard.

7. Kelvingrove Park
This wooded park is crossed by the Kelvin River.

8. Kelvingrove Art Museum
A must-see museum with stunning architecture.

9. Glasgow Science Centre
Features many interactive exhibitions.

10. The Lighthouse
A national centre for design and architecture
with 360° views over the city.

"

The Glasgow accent
was so strong you could
have built a bridge with
it and known it would
outlast the civilization
that spawned it.

"

Val McDermid

Glasgow is the only city in Scotland to have its own underground railway system.

Known affectionately as the "Clockwork Orange" due to the trains' colours, it is the third-oldest underground system in the world, beaten only by London and Budapest for age.

Dundee takes its name from two Celtic words: Dun means "fort", and "dee" may derive from the Celtic *dé*, meaning "fire".

The city is famously known for jute, jam and journalism.
The latter is still going strong – as well as being home to the creators of the *Beano* and the *Dandy* comic magazines, Dundee is also home to broadcasters like the BBC and STV.

"

This city [Dundee] will kill me. Halfway through my kipper this morning an enormous maggot crawled out and flashed his teeth at me.

"

Winston Churchill, who was an MP for Dundee between 1908 and 1922, in a letter to his wife, Clementine, from the Queen's Hotel.

As the jute industry exploded in Dundee in the 1800s, women outnumbered men in the mills by three to one – they were far cheaper to employ than men.

Unemployed Dundee men stayed at home, earning the scornful nickname "kettle bilers" (kettle boilers).

A small city, Dundee has incredible
achievements to its name:

Discovery of the **Horsehead Nebula**
in 1888 by born and bred Dundonian
astronomer, Williamina Fleming

Building of the **RRS Discovery** – the
world's first scientific research
ship – which in 1901, took Scott and
Shackleton to Antarctica.

Building **Mills Observatory**,
the first purpose-built observatory
in the UK.

Six Captivating Castles

Nowhere does castles quite like Scotland. From wonderfully preserved medieval strongholds to romantic clifftop ruins, here are six of the best.

Braemar Castle

Braemar, Ballater, Aberdeenshire

Built in 1628 for the Earl of Mar.

Blair Castle

Blair Atholl, Pitlochry, Perthshire

The ancient seat of the Dukes and Earls of Atholl.

Drummond Castle
Muthill, Crieff, Perthshire

17th-century castle with one of Europe's most impressive formal gardens.

Cawdor Castle
Cawdor, Nairn, Nairnshire

The romantic 14th-century home of the Thanes of Cawdor.

Eilean Donan Castle
Dornie, by Kyle of Lochalsh

Steeped in Jacobite lore with a picture-perfect setting.

Dunnottar Castle
Stonehaven, Aberddenshire

A formidable, cliff-top stronghold overlooking the north-east coast.

Nicknamed the "Granite City", Aberdeen is famous for its locally quarried granite stone.

It was used to build London's Houses of Parliament, Trafalgar Square and Waterloo Bridge, as well as Scotland's iconic Forth Rail Bridge.

Aberdeen has given its name
to more than 30 places across
the world.

There are 18 Aberdeens
in the US alone, and more in
Australia, Canada, Hong Kong,
India, Jamaica, Sierra Leone,
South Africa and Zimbabwe.

Aberdeenshire is home
to many wonderful castles,
the most famous of which
is probably the royal estate
of Balmoral – owned by the
British Royal Family
since 1852.

The **Brig O'Balgownie** –
Scotland's oldest bridge – spans
the River Don in Old Aberdeen.

It was completed in
1320, making it 700 years old.

It ceased to be a major route
in 1830 when the new Bridge of
Don was built downstream.

Britain's most northerly city is Inverness. The name comes from the Scottish Gaelic Inbhir Nis, which means "Mouth of the River Ness".

The city is a site of great geological interest as it lies on the Great Glen Fault. This fault line, a strike-slip fault, means that the rocks on each side of the line move in opposite directions.

Few tourist attractions in Scotland yank at the heartstrings in quite the same way as the Culloden Battlefield, the site of the last pitched battle to take place on British soil.

Fought near Inverness, the battle saw Jacobite forces meet a British army led by the Duke of Cumberland, son of the Hanoverian King George II. It was a bitter defeat for the Jacobites, with some 1,300 men slain.

CHAPTER
FIVE

KELPIES AND SELKIES

From brave warriors and cunning fairies to phantom pipers and fearsome beasts, the legends and lore of Scotland offer a glimpse into a world where magic and adventure abound.

From the Loch Ness Monster to the celebrated Stone of Scone, the country's rich and evocative stories have inspired artists, writers and poets for centuries.

Affectionately known as Nessie, the **Loch Ness Monster** has long captured the imagination of visitors to Scotland's beautiful Loch Ness. Over the years, there have been more than 1,100 recorded sightings of the creature in the loch's deep, dark waters.

Several sonar explorations have been undertaken to locate the creature, but none – so far – has been successful.

Reports of a monster inhabiting Loch Ness date back to ancient times. Local stone carvings depict a mysterious, flippered beast while the first written account appears in a biography of St Columba from 565 CE.

Mysterious, shapeshifting **Kelpies** are said to haunt Scotland's lochs and lonely rivers. The creature appears as a lost white or grey horse, and seems gentle and tame. But beware! Kelpies entice people to ride on their backs before taking them down to a watery grave.

In Falkirk, two giant horse-head sculptures celebrate the Kelpies. Standing 30 metres (98 feet) high, they are the largest equine sculptures in the world.

"

...When thowes dissolve
the snawy hoord
An' float the jinglin' icy boord
Then, water-kelpies haunt
the foord
By your direction
And 'nighted trav'llers
are allur'd
To their destruction...

"

Robert Burns, "Address to the Deil"

Selkies are shapeshifters, transforming between seal and human form by shedding and replacing their skin.

The selkie legend originated in the Orkney and Shetland Islands, where *selch* or *selk*(ie) is the Scots word for seal.

66

A good tale never tires in the telling.

99

Scottish proverb

Situated on the tiny island of Staffa, **Fingal's Cave** is formed entirely from hexagonally jointed basalt columns – a similar structure to the Giant's Causeway in Northern Ireland.

Nobody is sure how the cave got its name, but one legend tells how the Irish giant Finn McCool built the Giant's Causeway as a bridge between County Antrim and Scotland, so that he could cross the ocean without getting his feet wet.

Several stories of phantom pipers can be found in Scottish folklore.

At Culzean Castle, in South Ayrshire, a ghostly piper is said to herald any marriage in the Kennedy clan.

At Duntrune Castle, in Argyll, locals tell of how the haunting sounds of mysterious bagpipes sometimes echo across the waters of Loch Crinan.

Tales of ghostly **will-o'-the-wisps** have been told for centuries. These tiny, dancing flames – believed to be mischievous spirits of the dead – are said to flit across lonely bogs and marshes.

Legends tell of travellers being lured far from the safety of their paths and into danger.

"

Fantasy, myth, legend, truth – all are intertwined in the story that is Scotland.

"

Laurence Overmire

The **Big Grey Man** is said to haunt the summit and trails of Ben Macdui, the highest peak of the Cairngorms.

Described as being incredibly tall, with long arms and broad shoulders, the creature only ever appears under cover of mountain fog.

Some hikers have reported the sound of crunching gravel as the Grey Man moves stealthily through the gloom.

The legend of the **Stoor Worm** tells of a gigantic sea monster that terrorized the west coast of Scotland.

When it died, its huge teeth flew out and become the islands of Orkney, Shetland and the Faroes.

Fairies – or the **Wee Folk** – feature prominently in Scottish folklore.

There are many place names in Scotland named after the fairies such as Glen Shee (Fairy Glen) and Schiehallion (Fairy Hill of the Caledonians).

A type of Highland fairy called
a **loireag** was said to dwell
on the slopes of Beinn Mhòr,
South Uist's highest mountain.

Farmers dreaded her presence
as she cursed cattle so that
they couldn't move – only an
offering of milk or invoking
St Columba would chase
her away.

Six Spooky Spots

Mary King's Close, *The Royal Mile, Edinburgh*

Known as Scotland's spookiest street – and the
most haunted place in Edinburgh – Mary King's
Close was bricked up during an outbreak of the
plague and only recently reopened.

Fyvie Castle, *Fyvie, Aberdeenshire*

This castle is said to be haunted by the ghost
of Dame Lilias Drummond, who died there in
1601. A drummer and trumpeter are also believed
to haunt the castle.

Dunstaffnage Castle, *Dunbeg, Argyll and Bute*

Legend tells of a lady dressed in green who walks
the ramparts when momentous events are about
to unfold for the castle owners, Clan Campbell.

Abbotsford House, *Melrose, Roxburghshire*

The former home of Sir Walter Scott, this house has a long history of ghostly activity – with Sir Walter himself even reporting unnerving happenings.

Culloden Moor, *Culloden, Inverness*

The site of one of the most infamous battles in British history, this atmospheric moor is said to be plagued by the ghosts of those who perished there.

Glamis Castle, *Forfar, Angus*

The childhood home of Lady Elizabeth Bowes-Lyon – later, the Queen Mother – this castle, set against the stunning Grampian mountains, is said to be haunted by at least six restless souls.

The Stone of Scone

Also known as the Stone of Destiny, this ancient stone was used for centuries in the coronation ceremonies of Scottish monarchs. Taken to England several times over the centuries, it was returned to Scotland in 1996 and is now on display in Edinburgh Castle.

According to legend, it was used as a pillow by Jacob in the Old Testament, and brought to Scotland by way of Egypt, Spain and Ireland.

66

Unless the fates be
faulty grown
And prophet's voice be vain
Where'er is found this
sacred stone
The Scottish race shall reign.

99

**The inscription (translated by Sir Walter Scott
in 1620) that was allegedly on a metal plaque attached
to the Stone of Scone**

On the beautiful Isle of Lewis, legend tells of the **Blue Men of the Minch** or **Storm Kelpies**.

Living just below the water's surface, these creatures like to stir up a storm — quite literally.

In Celtic mythology, a white stag is often associated with otherworldly or magical powers.

Seeing a solitary white stag, or hart, is said to be a very lucky occurrence that will bring good fortune for the rest of a person's life.

CHAPTER

SIX

SECRET SCOTLAND

Beyond the big sights and well-known facts, Scotland is a land of surprises.

Did you know that the unicorn has been a symbol of Scotland for centuries, or that the beautiful Isle of Skye is home to an extrodinary collection of mid-Jurassic dinosaur footprints?

Read on to discover just a few of Scotland's wonderful secrets.

The **unicorn** has been
used as a symbol of Scotland
for centuries.

The mythical creature is often
shown on the Scottish coat of
arms, where it represents purity,
grace and strength.

"

But Edinburgh is a mad god's dream
Fitful and dark,
Unseizable in Leith
And wildered by the Forth,
But irresistibly at last
Cleaving to sombre heights
Of passionate imagining
Till stonily,
From soaring battlements,
Earth eyes Eternity.

"

These words, by Scottish poet Hugh MacDiarmid (1892-1978), appear on the wall of the Scottish Parliament.

Scotland has over
790 offshore islands,
making it one of
the most island-rich
countries in the world.

Only 30 of these
are inhabited.

On the island of Jura, red deer outnumber people by 30 to one!

The world's first colour photograph – of a tartan ribbon – was taken by Scottish mathematician James Clerk Maxwell in 1861.

It now resides in a small museum at 14 India Street, Edinburgh, the house where Maxwell was born.

The **Falkirk Wheel** is the world's only rotating boat lift. An exceptional feat of modern engineering, it connects the Forth & Clyde and Union Canals.

Boats are lifted by a height of 35 metres (115 feet) to bridge the gap that was originally linked by a flight of 11 locks.

The world's first paramedic service was established in Glasgow, in 1865.

The innovative system, which relied on horse-drawn ambulances and trained paramedics, helped to improve the delivery of medical care and set a standard for future ambulance services.

Covering a distance of just 1.7 miles, the flight between Westray and Papa Westray — two small islands in the Orkney archipelago — is one of the shortest scheduled flights in the world.

Lasting just two minutes, the flight is considered a vital connection for the island communities and provides an important link to the mainland.

The dramatic **Corryvreckan Whirlpool** – situated between the islands of Jura and Scarba off the west coast of mainland Scotland – is the third largest whirlpool in the world.

At full strength, the currents can reach over 10 knots and produce waves over 9 metres (30 feet) high.

If you're feeling brave, daily boat trips run to the site.

Scotland is home to the
tallest waterfall in Britain,
Eas a' Chual Aluinn.

With a sheer drop of
200 metres (660 feet), it is
three times the height of
Niagara Falls when
in full flow.

In 1823, Glaswegian scientist Charles Macintosh invented a method for making waterproof garments by using rubber dissolved in coal-tar naphtha for cementing two pieces of cloth together.

The mackintosh – or "mac" – was named for him.

"

Today's rain is
tomorrow's whisky.

"

Scottish saying

"

In Scotland, when people congregate, they tend to argue and discuss and reason; in Orkney, they tell stories.

"

George Mackay Brown

66

Scotland is the country
above all others that I
have seen, in which a man
of imagination may carve
out his own pleasures;
there are so many
inhabited solitudes.

99

Dorothy Wordsworth

The **Fortingall Yew** stands within Fortingall churchyard, in Perthshire.

It is thought to be between 3,000 and 9,000 years old and has connections to early Christianity in Scotland.

It is also believed to be one of the oldest living things in Europe.

The Isle of Skye has earned
a reputation as the "Dinosaur Isle".
A staggering collection of footprints
has been discovered there dating back
to the mid-Jurassic period.

Most of them belong to giant
sauropods, but a recent discovery at
Brother's Point confirms the island was
also home to hefty meat-eaters.

Scotland has three official languages – English, Scots and Scottish Gaelic.

99 per cent of the population speak English and 1 percent speak Scottish Gaelic. Of the English speakers, around 30 per cent use the Scots dialect – which derives from Old English but has a number of unique regional words.

Edinburgh's iconic Princes Street was part of the New Town plan designed by James Craig in 1767. It was planned for the street to be named after the patron saint of Edinburgh, St Giles.

However, King George III objected – since St Giles is also the patron saint of lepers – and he decided the street would be named after his two sons, the princes.

Scotland's national flag – the St Andrew's Cross or Saltire – is believed to be the oldest flag in Europe.

66

It was the beauty of the country before them that had done it. Scotland was a place of attenuated light, of fragility, of a beauty that broke the heart.

99

Alexander McCall Smith,
Love in the Time of Bertie, 2022

"

Haste ye back!

"

Traditional Scottish saying